Lines

compiled by
Charles Keller

illustrated by
Christine Randall

10 9 8 7 6 5 4 3 2 1
Copyright © 1974 by Charles Keller
Illustrations copyright © 1974 by Prentice-Hall
All rights reserved. No part of this book may be reproduced in any form or by any means, except for the inclusion of brief quotations in a review, without permission in writing from the publisher.

Printed in the United States of America • J

Prentice-Hall International, Inc., London
Prentice-Hall of Australia, Pty. Ltd., North Sydney
Prentice-Hall of Canada, Ltd., Toronto
Prentice-Hall of India Private Ltd., New Delhi
Prentice-Hall of Japan, Inc., Tokyo

Library of Congress Cataloging in Publication Data

Keller, Charles.
   Laugh lines.

   SUMMARY: A collection from American folklore of jokes the reader can draw, including picture puzzles, story riddles, and catch tales.
   1. Wit and humor, Juvenile. [1. Joke books. 2. Wit and humor] I. Randall, Christine, illus. II. Title.
PZ8.7.K42Lau   73-13979
ISBN 0-13-526038-8

table of contents

catch tales 7
story riddles 17
picture puzzles 41

The Monkeys, the Banana Tree and the River

Once there was a river with a bridge running across it. On one side was a banana tree. On the other side was a Mama monkey and her baby monkey. They were hungry, so the Mama monkey crossed the bridge to the banana tree. But while she was there, the river flooded suddenly and wiped out the bridge. Now the question is, how can the little monkey get across the river and join his mother and have some bananas?

Well, if a big monkey like you can't figure it out, how do you expect the little one to?

Two Donkeys

Two donkeys were tied to a tree. Twenty feet away was a bale of hay. One donkey was tied with a rope 15 feet long, and the other was tied with a rope 10 feet long. How did the donkeys get to the hay? Do you give up?
That's exactly what the other two jackasses did.

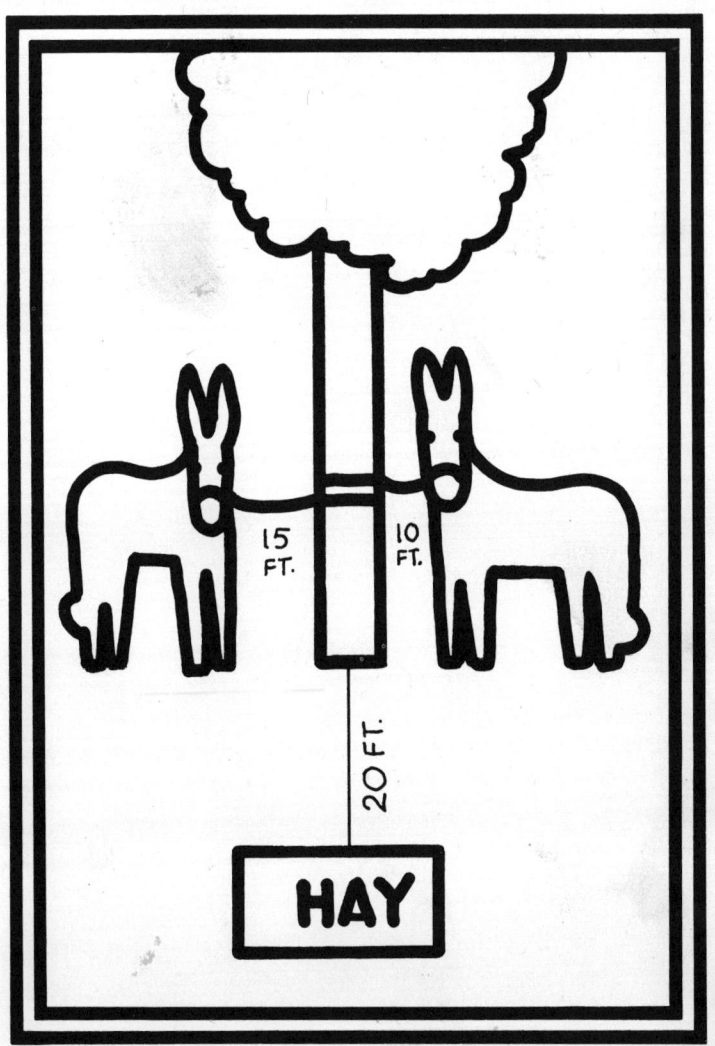

The Lunch

A girl had a dollar for lunch. She bought a bottle of soda for 20¢, a bag of potato chips for 10¢, but she still needed a sandwich. Ham sandwiches were 80¢, roast beef was 85¢ and salami was 75¢. What kind of sandwich did she get?
Baloney, just like you're getting.

The Boy and the Burglar

A boy woke up to see a shadow 8 feet long. It was 40 feet from his bed. The burglar making the shadow was 4 feet tall, with legs 2 feet long. He could move at the rate of 8 feet a second. He was 20 feet from the window. The boy was 22 feet from the window. How did the boy catch the burglar?

He pulled his leg, just like I'm pulling yours.

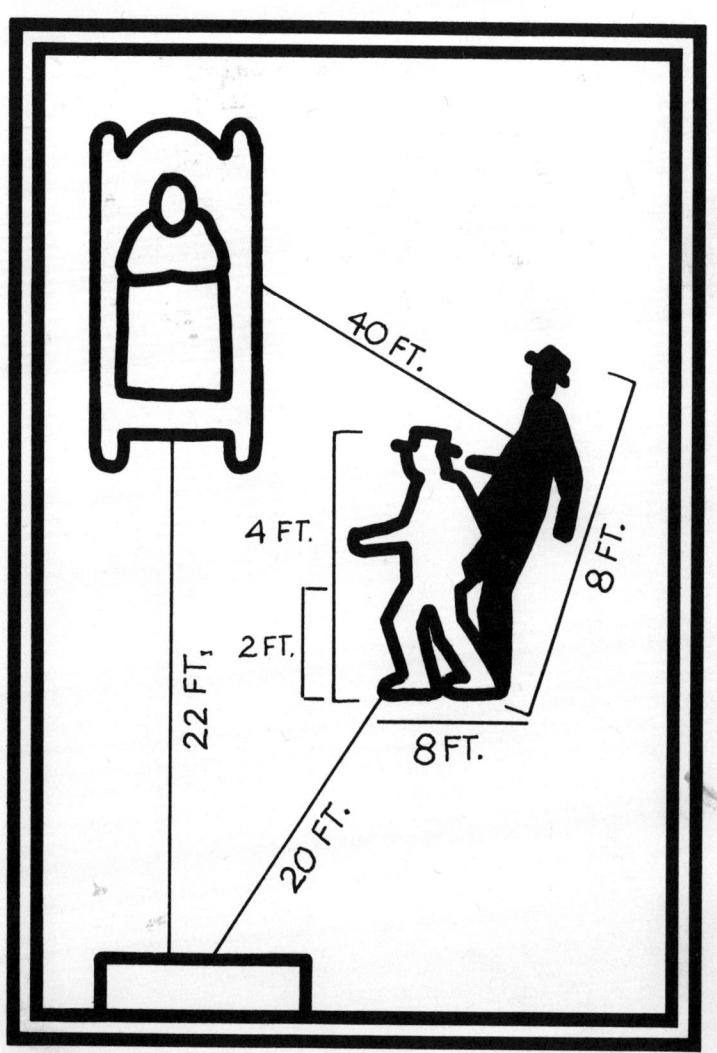

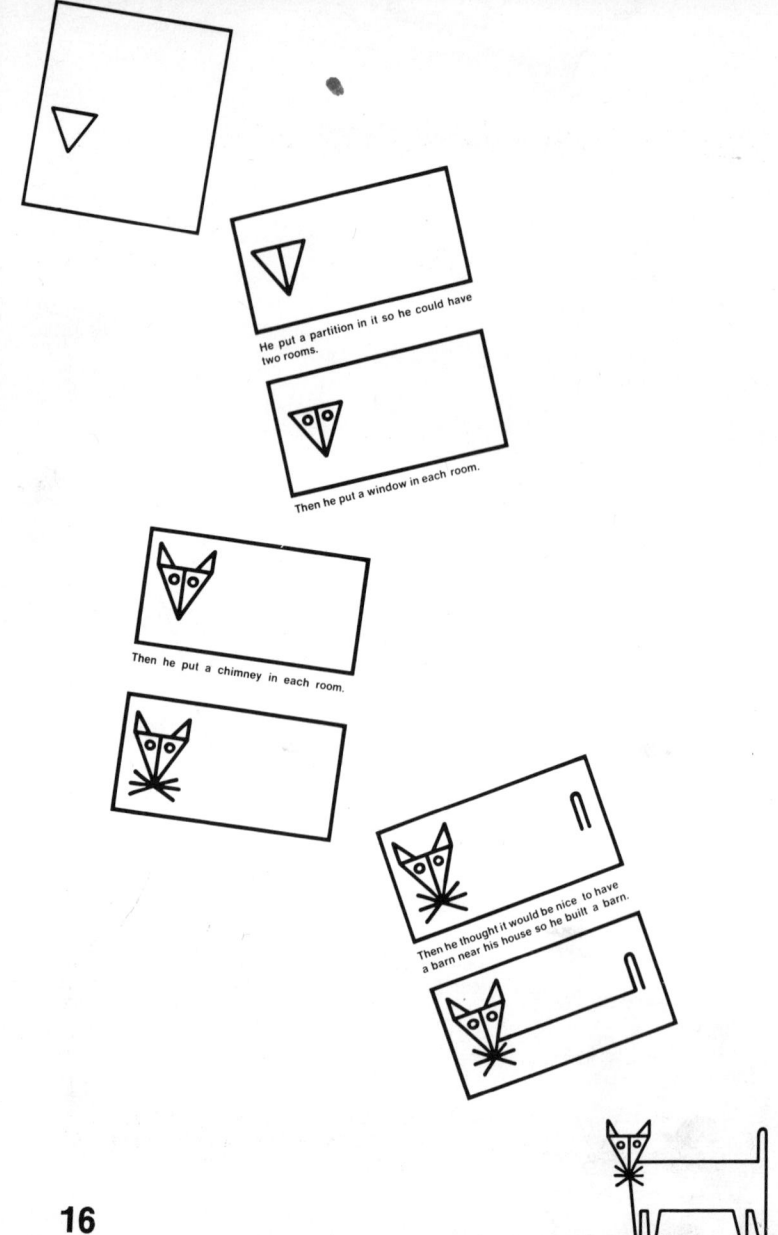

The Hunter and the Lion

A hunter went hunting for a lion with two bullets in his gun.

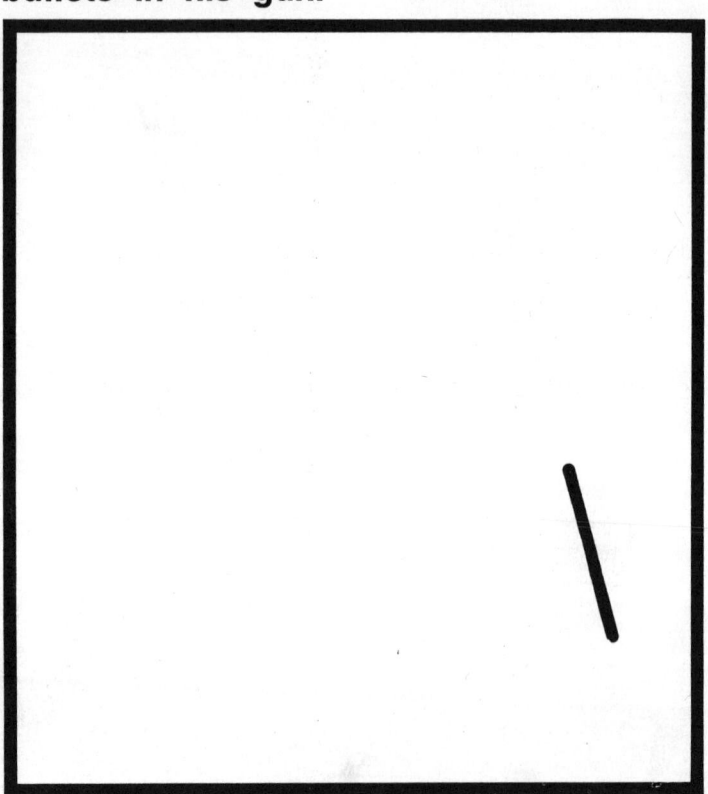

He walked into the jungle.

He went to the valley where the lions are.

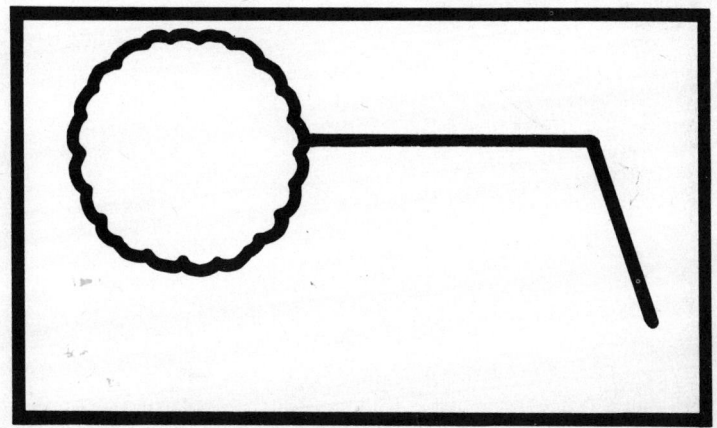

He heard a loud roar.

He planted his feet firmly on the ground and saw the lion in the distance.

The lion charged. He fired and missed and the lion ran back.

He moved to a new position to get closer to the lion.

The lion charged again. He fired again and missed and the lion retreated.

He had no more bullets left so he left the jungle.
Who is still the king of the jungle?

The Boy's Pet

Can you guess what kind of pet this boy had?

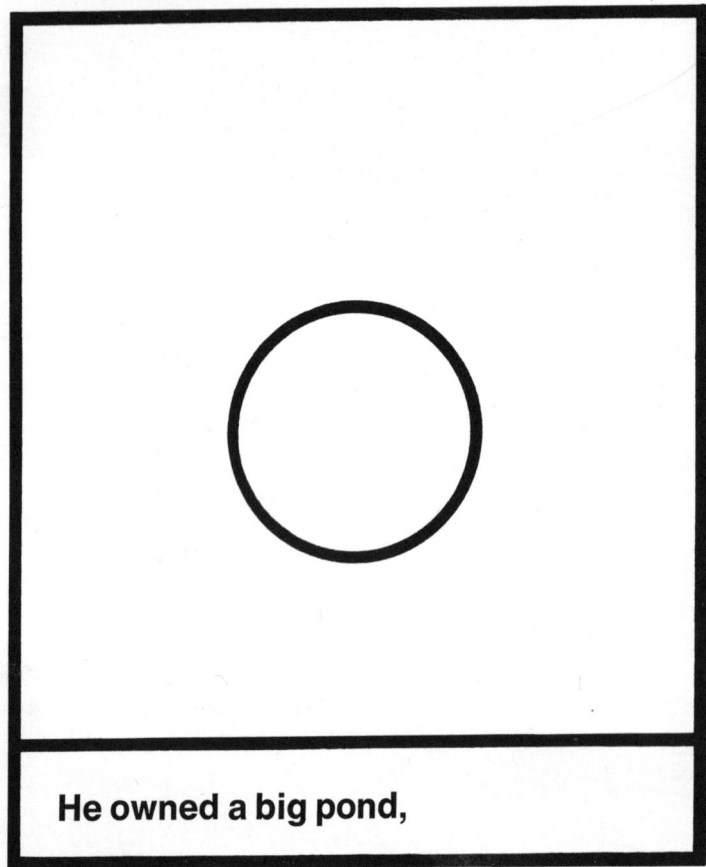

He owned a big pond,

with a grassy island in it.

Cattails grew at one end of the pond.

He lived in a house with one window nearby.

He shook his rug out of the door.

There was a path that went from his house to the pond.

Two Indians lived in tents and came up two paths each day for water.

**What was the boy's pet?
A big bird.**

The Wild Cat

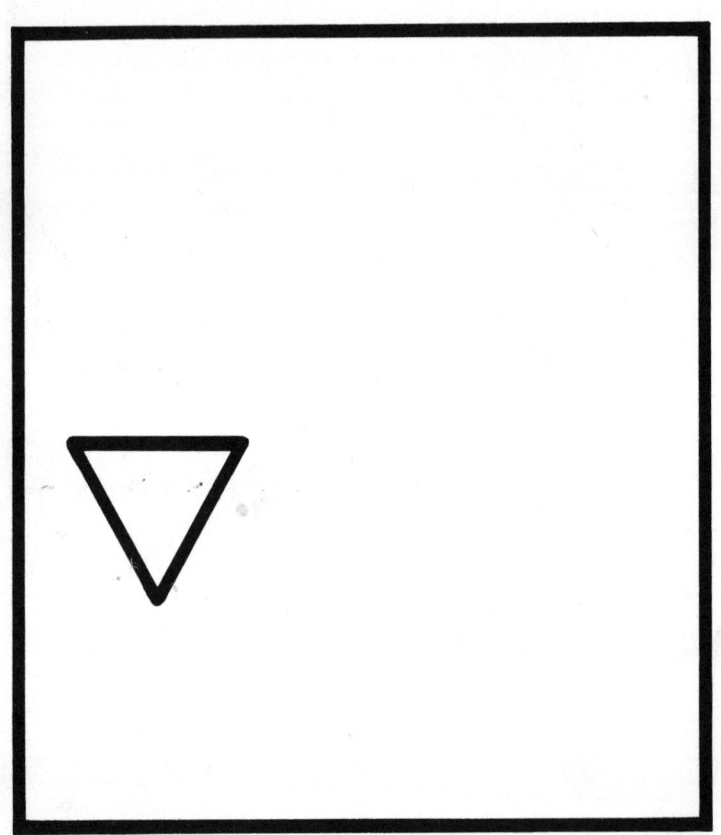

Once there was an old man who built himself a house. This is how he built it.

He put a partition in it so he could have two rooms.

Then he put a window in each room.

Then he put a chimney in each room.

Then he planted some grass beside the door.

The Lost Bicycle

One morning a boy discovered that his bicycle was missing.

He circled the block to look for it.

He didn't find it so he went to all his friends' houses to look for it.

He looked up and down that corner.

He then circled that block looking for it.

**He checked every back yard.
He found it.**

picture puzzles

what's this?

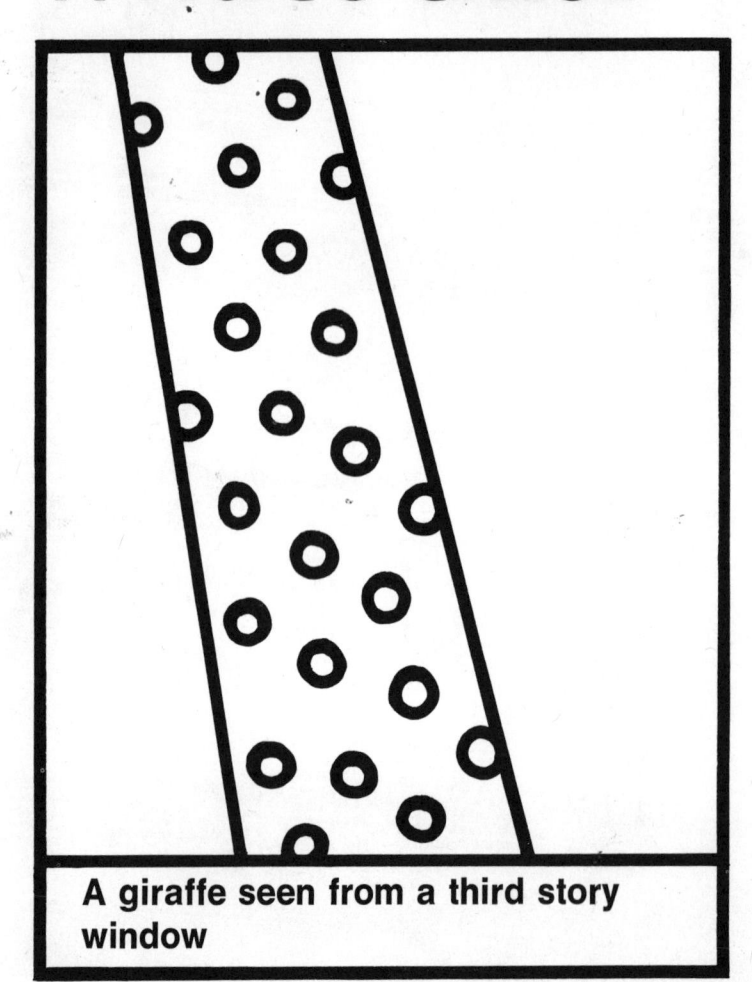

A giraffe seen from a third story window

The early worm catching the bird

what's this?

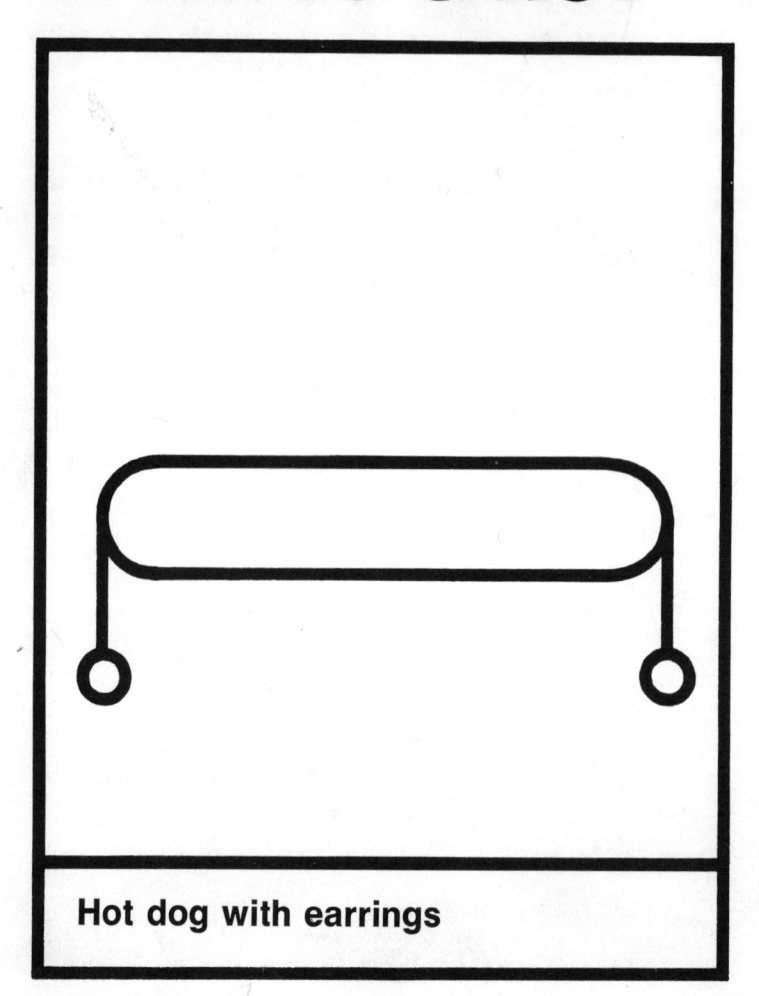

Hot dog with earrings

A cowboy frying an egg

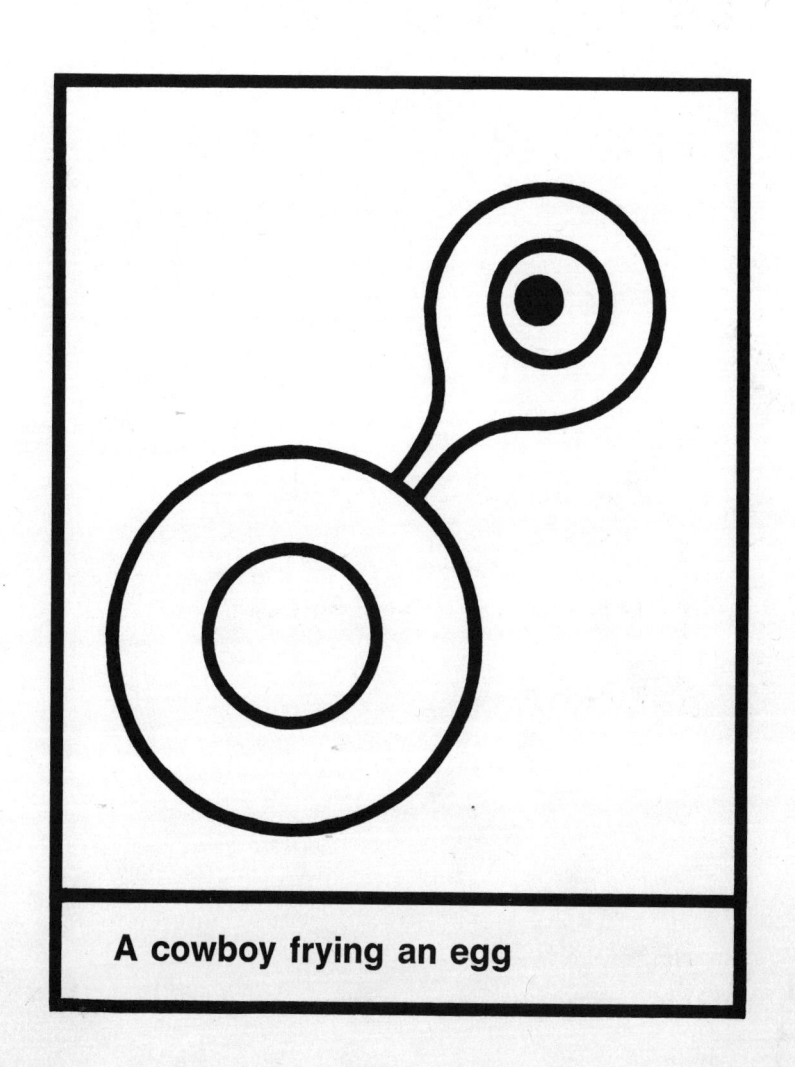

what's this?

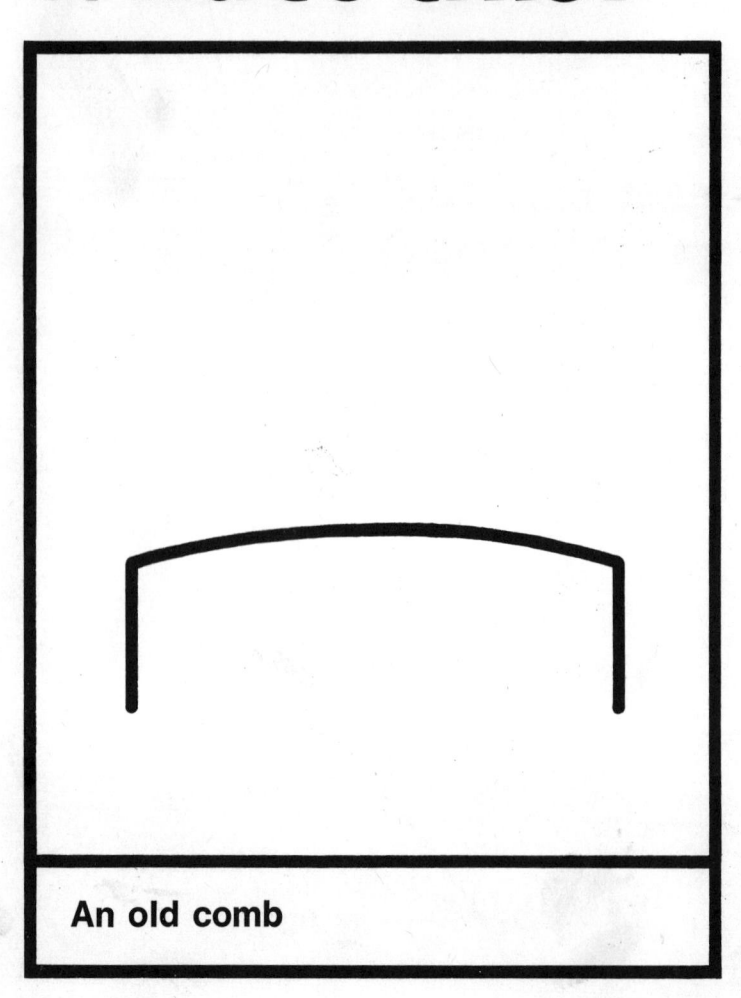

An old comb

A two carrot ring

what's this?

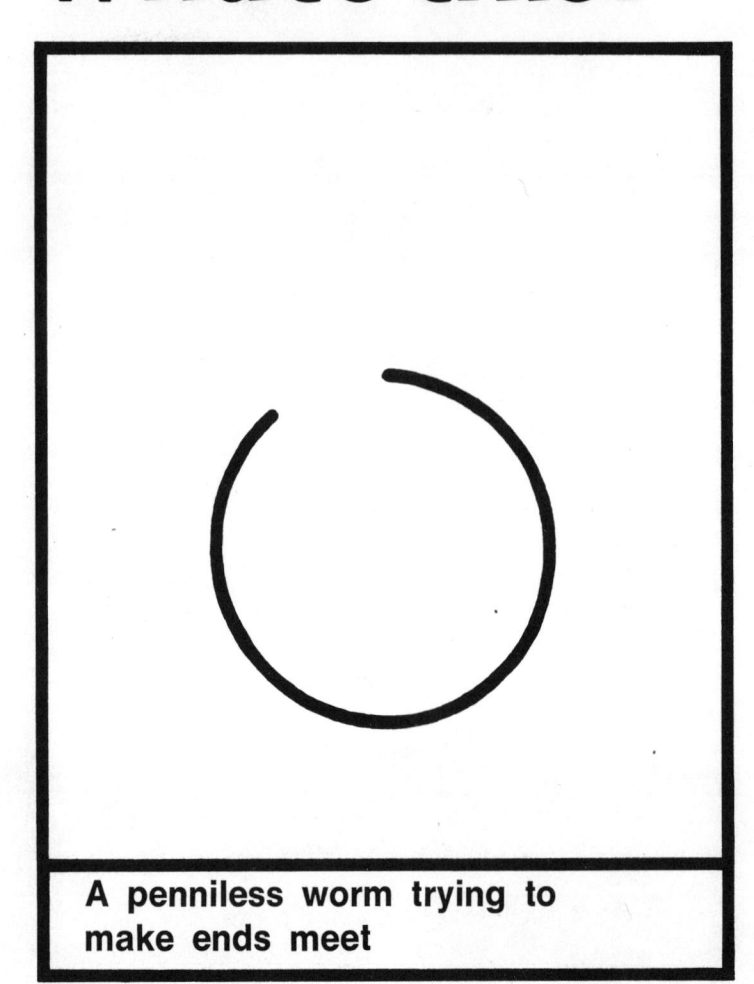

A penniless worm trying to make ends meet

Highway for grasshoppers

what's this?

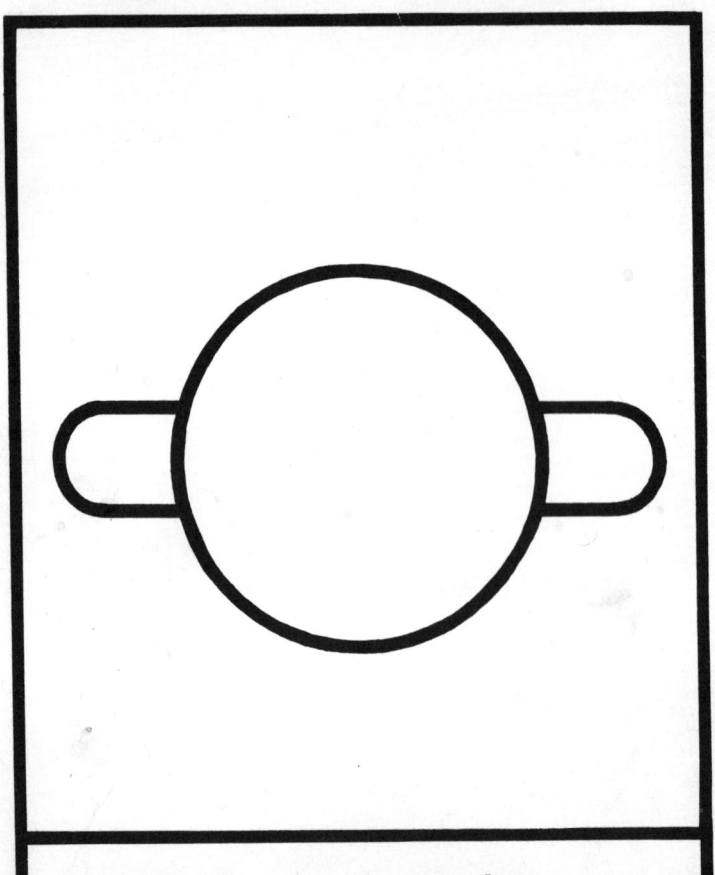

A hotdog in a hamburger bun

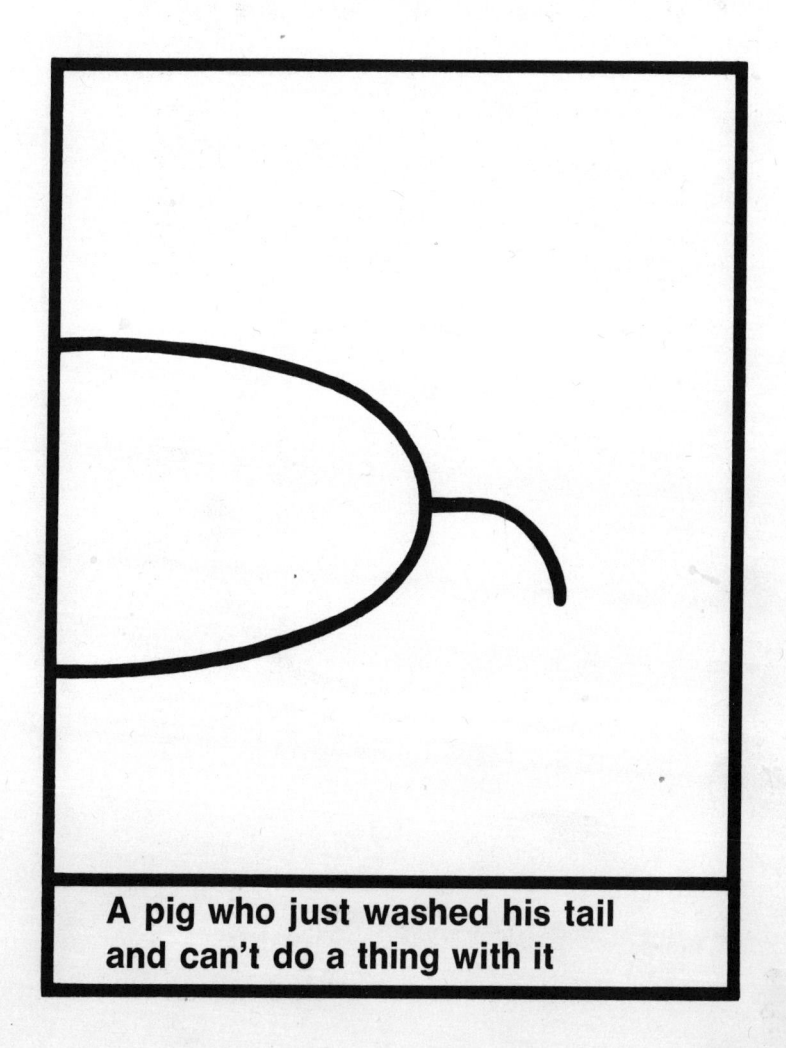

A pig who just washed his tail and can't do a thing with it

what's this?

A teethpick

Boy stepping on gum

what's this?

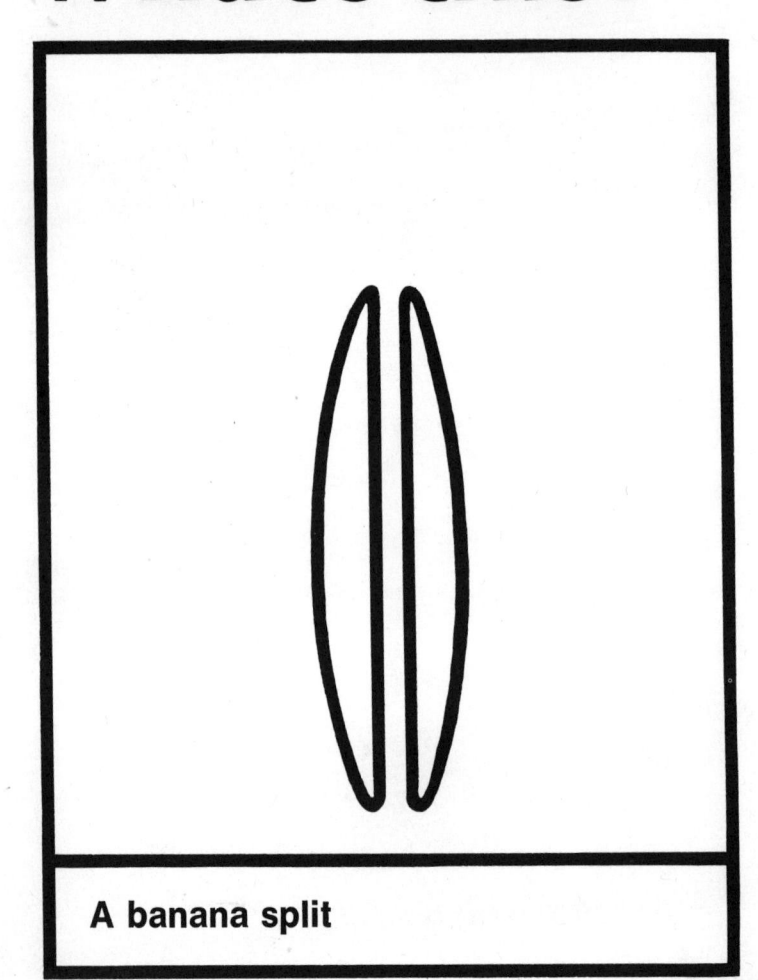

A banana split

Two birds fighting over worm

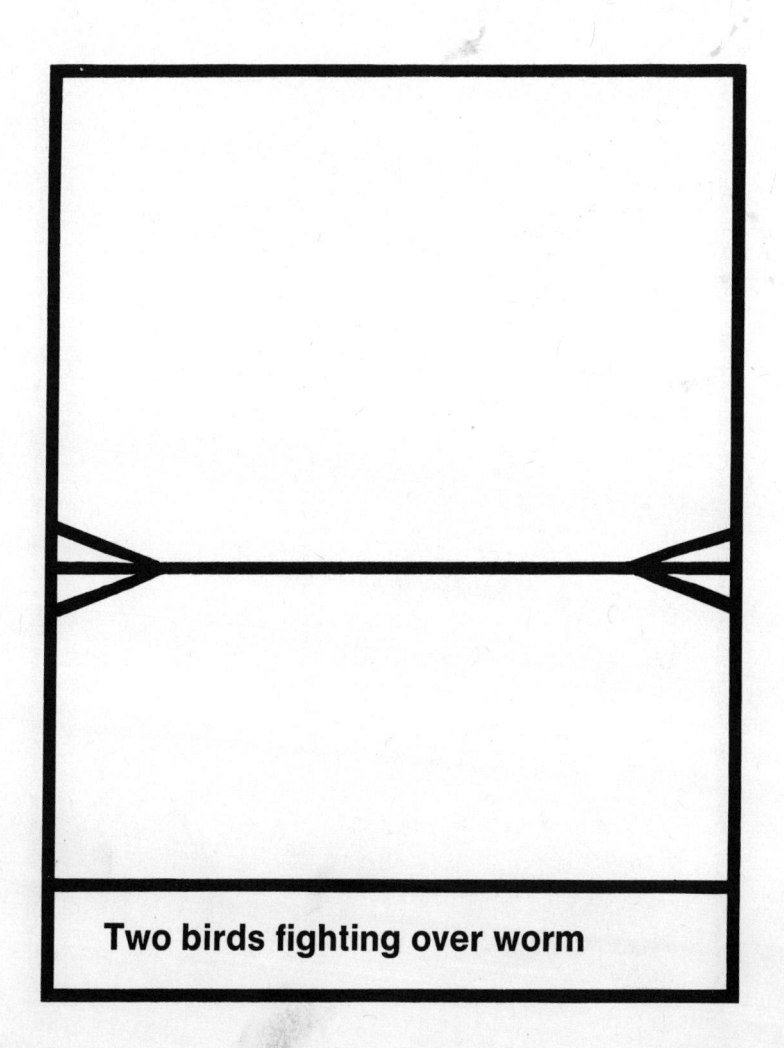

what's this?

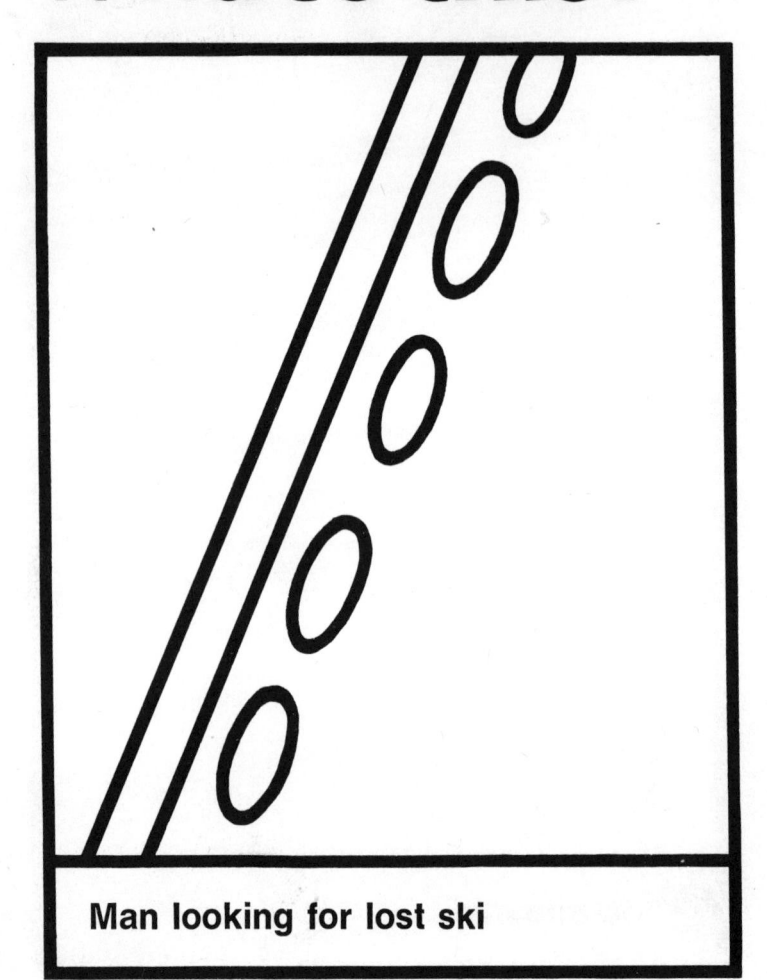

Man looking for lost ski

Polar bear in snowstorm

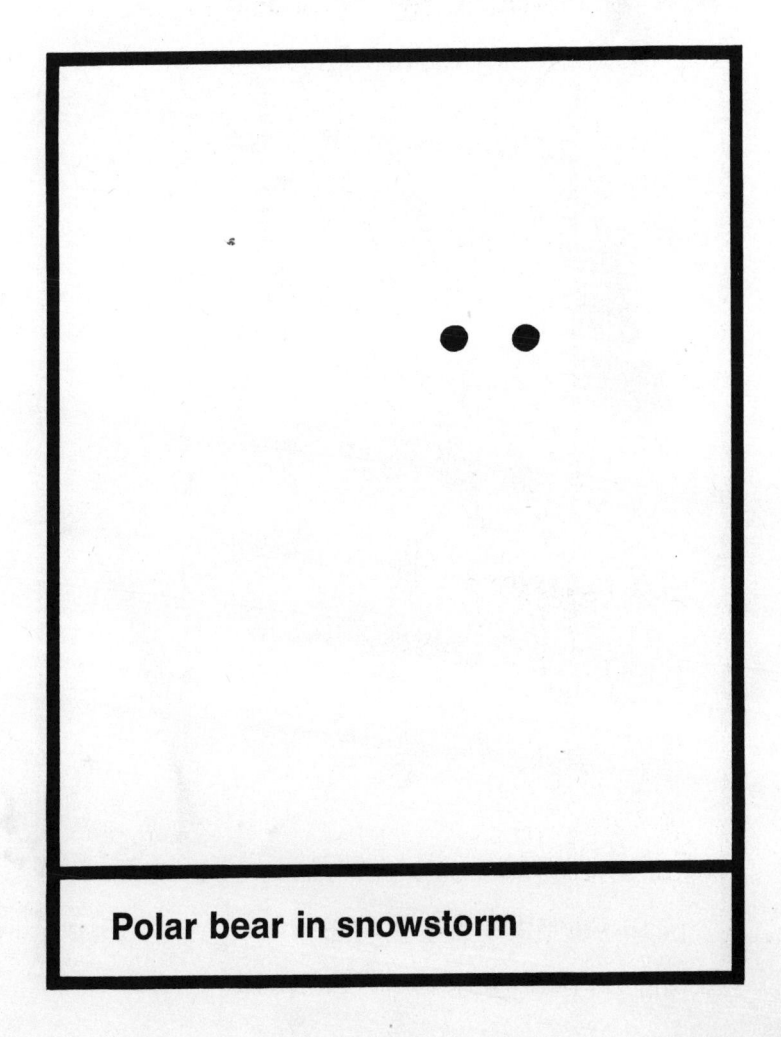

what's this?

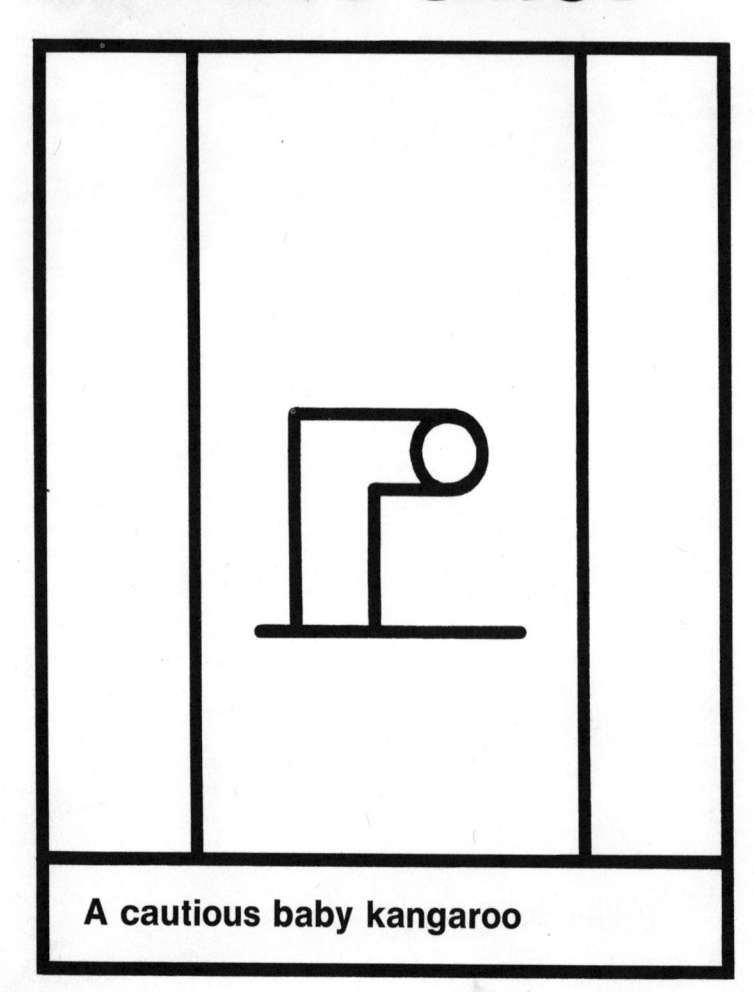

A cautious baby kangaroo

Ex-sheriff's badge

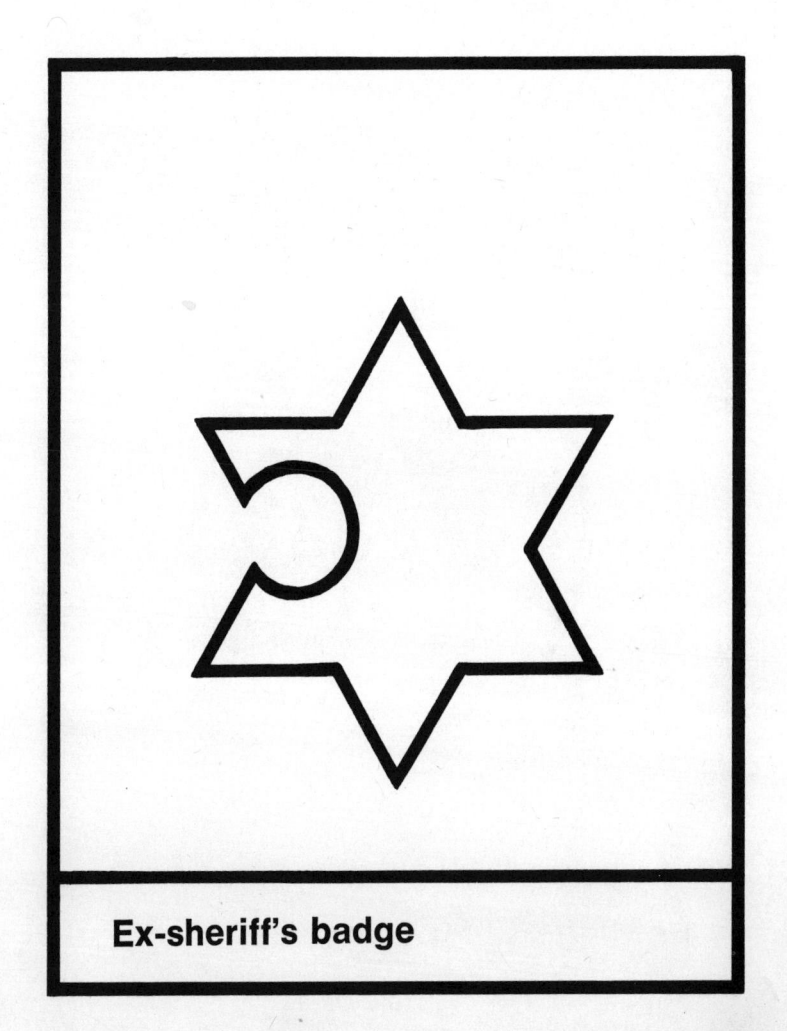

what's this?

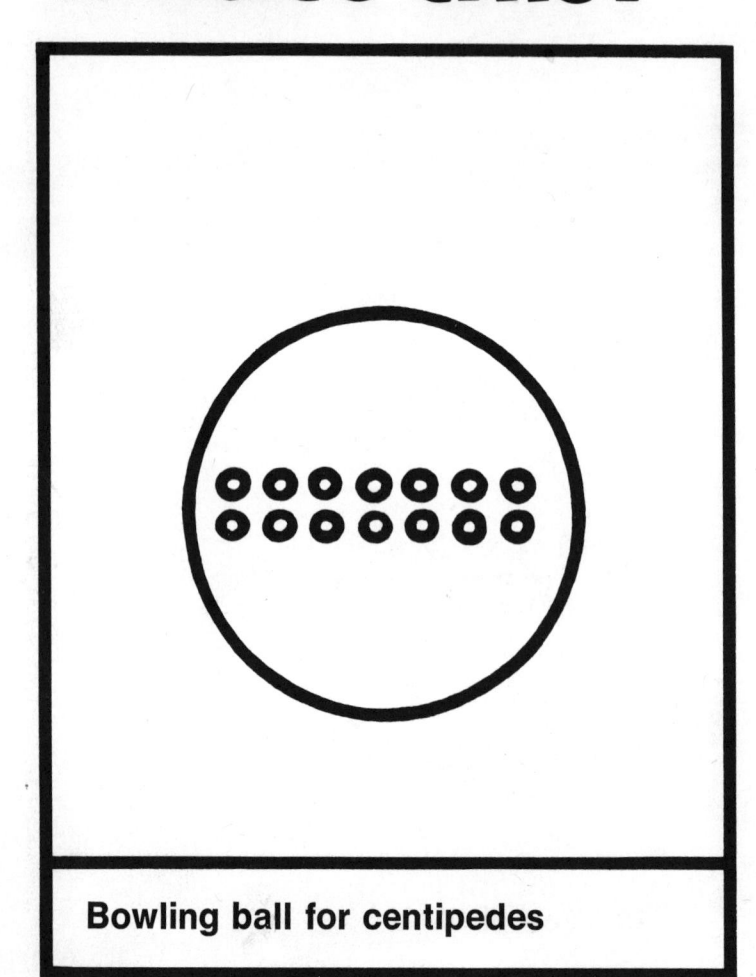

Bowling ball for centipedes

Octopus at attention

what's this?

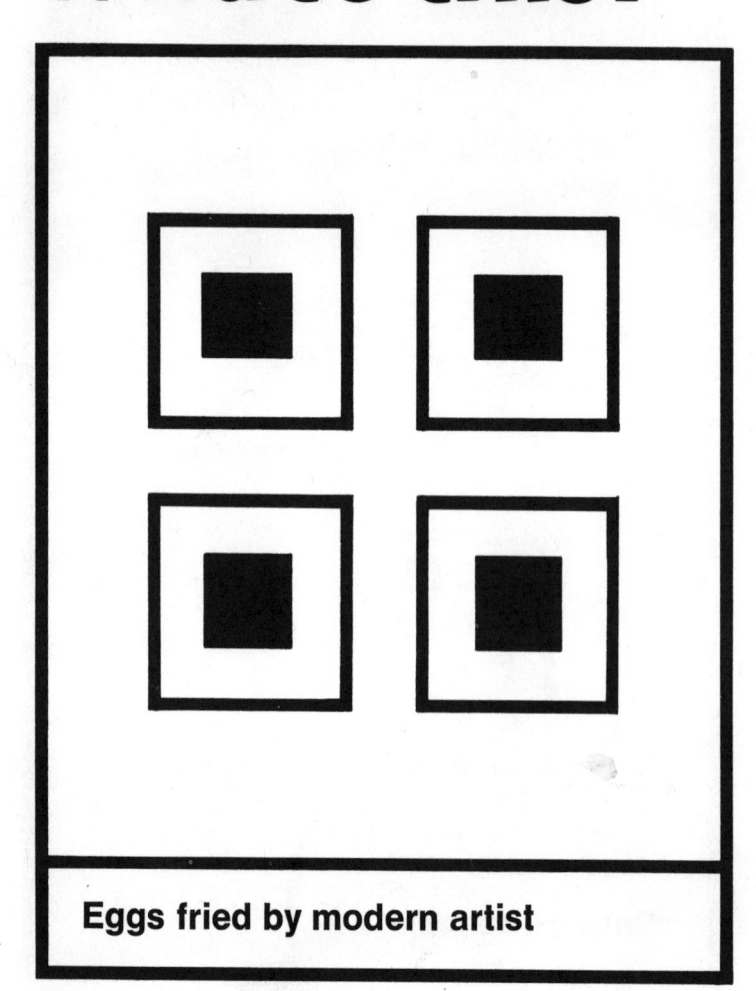

Eggs fried by modern artist

Famous last words of a skin-diver

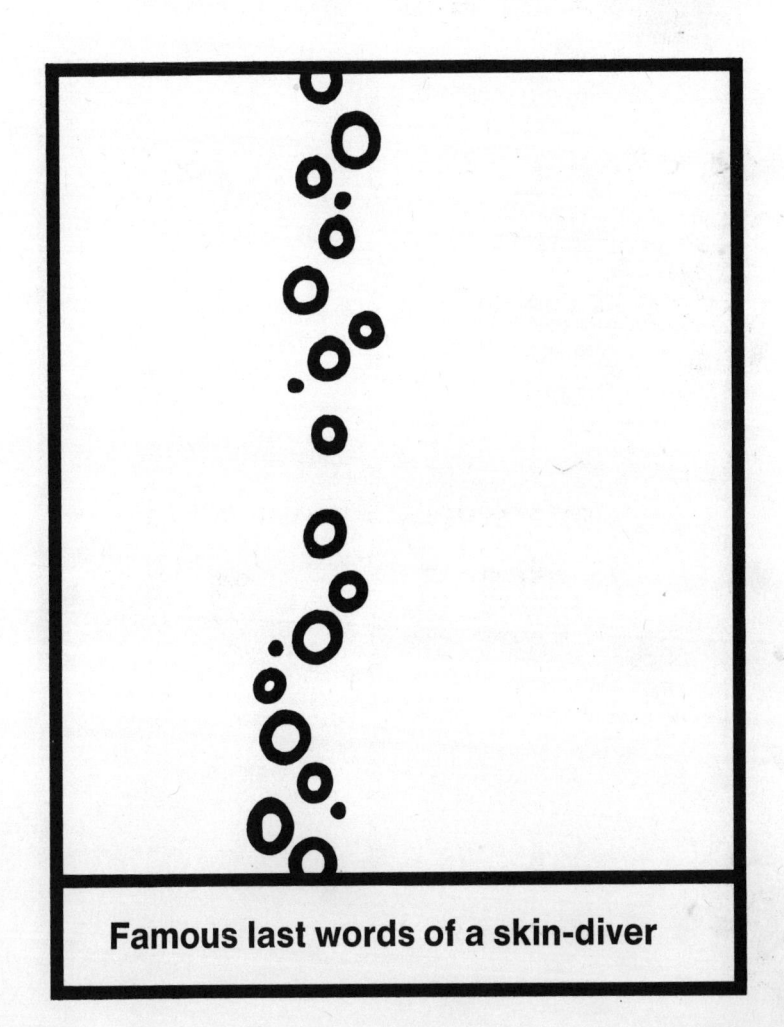

what's this?

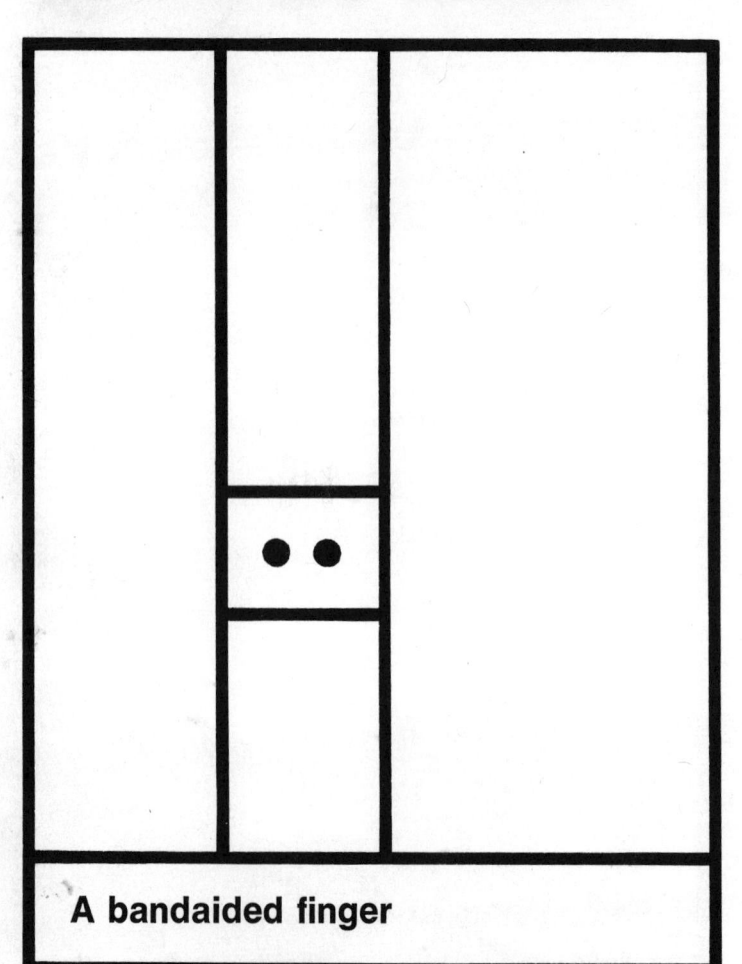

A bandaided finger